Original title:
Saplings and Snickers

Copyright © 2025 Creative Arts Management OÜ
All rights reserved.

Author: Vivienne Beaumont
ISBN HARDBACK: 978-1-80567-421-4
ISBN PAPERBACK: 978-1-80567-720-8

Nature's Serenade and Ticklish Joy

In a garden full of cheer,
Little sprouts peek out, it's clear.
Twirling leaves, they dance so bold,
Whispers of laughter, stories told.

Fluttering bugs join the fun,
Chasing shadows in the sun.
Tiny voices make a cheer,
What a joyful atmosphere!

Gentle Joys of the Earth

The daisies wear a silly hat,
While the clover whispers, 'What's up, cat?'
A busy bee, like a tiny car,
Buzzing heedlessly, here and far.

Wiggly worms tell jokes so sly,
Underneath the open sky.
Planting smiles in the dirt,
Who knew mud could be dessert?

Frolicsome Roots and Lighthearted Thoughts

Roots burrow deep, then reach for fun,
Cracking jokes under the sun.
A pebble giggles as it rolls,
Whispering secrets to the shoals.

Grass tickles toes in a playful way,
While butterflies flutter in ballet.
Nature's jesters, all around,
Jovial spirits can be found.

Giggling Gardens and Verdant Dreams

In fields where wild giggles grow,
Nature's wonders steal the show.
Sunlight streams through leafy greens,
Painting scenes like crazy beans.

Petals bounce with every gust,
Creating laughter, it's a must!
The world wears joy, a bright parade,
In this garden, dreams aren't delayed!

Sunshine's Embrace and Joyful Steps

In the garden, giggles sprout,
Tiny leaves, no doubt they pout,
Bouncing balls and playful beams,
Whispers of the sun's bright dreams.

Chasing shadows, grass beneath,
Every tumble, blissful wreath,
Daisy chains in tangled hair,
Laughter dances in the air.

Nature's Joust and Gleeful Play

Bugs in armor, brave and bold,
In the wild, their tales unfold,
Worms in races, swift and sly,
Try to catch the buzzing fly.

While the frogs do leap and croak,
Chasing tails of teasing smoke,
Nature's jesters, full of cheer,
Turning moments into years.

Heartfelt Flourish and Jovial Hideaways

Underneath the leafy roof,
Tiny giggles steal the proof,
Hidden spots where shadows play,
Whimsy rules the light of day.

Squirrels wear their acorn hats,
Cheeky chatter — just like chats,
While the breeze in whirlwinds swings,
Nature sings of silly things.

Sprightly Greens and Joyful Tunes

In the meadow, music swells,
Every flower, a story tells,
Running happily, feet so free,
Twirling petals, wild and spree.

Dandelions blow with flare,
Whirling seeds, a fancied air,
Laughter echoes through the scene,
Life's a dance, a playful dream.

Sunlit Wonders and Cheery Chimes

In the garden, giggles sprout,
Tiny roots give a playful shout,
Leaves twist like a merry dance,
Who knew a plant could take a chance?

Bugs wear hats, the ants parade,
Flowers laugh in the sun's cascade,
Twirling vines, in bloom and jest,
Nature's comedy, at its best.

Gentle Breezes and Playful Dreams

Breezes fluff the grass so neat,
Tickling toes, what a treat!
Dandelions puff with cheer,
As whispers of laughter draw near.

A squirrel in a funny twist,
Tries to dance, but can't resist,
Chasing shadows, what a sight,
The world's a stage, pure delight!

Whimsical Green Tales

In a patch where mushrooms talk,
Joking loudly as they walk,
Toadstools giggle with delight,
Under the glow of the moonlight.

Frogs play pranks on sleeping snails,
While a breeze carries cartoon tales,
Laughter echoes through the land,
Green enchantments, ever so grand.

The Sound of Leaves in Joy

Leaves rustle like a giggling crowd,
Whispers shout, "Come join the loud!"
Each flutter tells a joke or two,
Nature's laughter, bright and true.

Branches stretch for a ticklish breeze,
Bouncing twigs dance with such ease,
Nestled critters chime along,
Life's a joke, a happy song.

Soft Beginnings and Joyous Revelry

Tiny shoots in the ground,
Wiggly worms all around.
They dance with a little tune,
Beneath the bright, silver moon.

Frogs croak with glee, oh what fun,
Playing tag with the warm sun.
Every leaf shakes and sways,
In laughter that brightens the days.

Fresh Form and Spirited Fun

Little sprouts stretch up high,
Bouncing under a baby sky.
Squirrels chuckle, what a sight,
As they twirl and take flight.

Bright petals stick out their tongues,
Giggles spill from all the young.
The breeze tickles every face,
In this joyous, lively place.

Childlike Wonder and Nature's Chuckles

With every seed that starts to grow,
Comes a laugh, oh don't you know?
Sunshine whispers silly games,
While bees buzz and call their names.

Tiny critters play peek-a-boo,
As the wind sings just for you.
Dandelions blow, seeds like fluff,
Wishing well, isn't this fun enough?

Laughing Roots in Sunlit Groves

Roots giggle deep in the earth,
Sharing secrets of their birth.
With every wiggle, a new joke lands,
All is bright in these playful bands.

Light dances on the leafy tips,
As frogs leap and do little flips.
Nature's joy cannot be tamed,
In this world, we'd never be blamed.

Newborn Growth and Gentle Chuckles

Tiny seeds push through the ground,
Wobbling leaves, oh what a sound!
With every sprout, a giggle flows,
As they dance in rows and rows.

A little breeze gives them a shake,
Tickling roots with each little quake.
They sway and sway, a funny show,
Making sunlight their best amigo.

The Joyful Tickle of Earth

Under soil, a laugh does bloom,
Worms in laughter, wiggle and zoom.
Tiny buds with their leafy grins,
Count all the chuckles, oh what wins!

Raindrops fall with a splashy cheer,
Each drop a joke that all can hear.
As flowers stretch, they share the light,
Raising giggles, what a delight!

Breezy Whimsy Among Young Branches

Branches twist in a playful breeze,
Shaking off droplets with such ease.
Each leaf whispers a quirk or two,
In the laughter of skies so blue.

A squirrel jumps with a silly pout,
Trying to find what it's all about.
Giggling buds wave hello and bye,
As bumblebees buzz merrily by.

Frolics in the Woodland Playground

In the woods, where young things play,
Laughter leaps from day to day.
Leaves make jokes in the dappled light,
As shadows mock in friendly sight.

A rabbit hops, its ears take flight,
Chasing breezes, a comical sight.
With every turn, a chuckle grows,
In this realm where whimsy flows.

Beneath the Canopy's Giggle

Under the leafy cheer,
Little critters dancing near,
Bouncing on their tiny toes,
Nature's laughter freely flows.

Chasing shadows, playing trick,
Watch out now, the branches flick,
With every giggle, joy unfolds,
Wacky stories nature holds.

Sunbeams peek through, what a sight,
Twinkling leaves, oh what delight,
Frogs croak jokes, the squirrels tease,
All around, the world just fees.

A breeze whispers a cheerful tune,
Laughter echoes 'neath the moon,
In this playhouse green and bright,
Giggling buds greet the night.

Laughter Among Young Leaves

In the garden, young and spry,
Laughter dances in the sky,
Birds crack jokes, oh what fun,
Sunshine happy, everyone.

Leaves swirl in a playful game,
Every rustle calls a name,
Laughing flowers, bright and bold,
Nature's tales are sweetly told.

Bumblebees buzz, adding flair,
With little giggles everywhere,
The world feels light, just like a breeze,
Joyful moments put us at ease.

Night descends, the giggles stay,
In soft whispers, they softly play,
Among the young, so wild and free,
Life's a joke, come laugh with me!

Sprouts of Joy in the Forest

Sprouts peek up, all bright and green,
In the woods, quite a scene,
Whispers tickle the playful bark,
Every nook hides a little spark.

Tickled trunks and twirling vines,
Nature knows how to redefine,
Silly shadows prance around,
Rippling giggles in their sound.

Bunny hops with a joyful skip,
While owls share secrets, never drip,
Laughter bounces, trying to hide,
As leaves sway with the giggling tide.

Underneath the starlit sky,
All the creatures chime and sigh,
In this forest, pure delight,
Joy blooms brightly, day and night.

Whispers of Green and Glee

Little sprouts begin to laugh,
In the wild, they find their path,
With a wiggle and a bounce,
Each new grin, they must announce.

Ticklish petals close their eyes,
As the wind tells funny lies,
Rustling branches giggle too,
In this glee, we're all brand new.

Sunlight spots hold little treats,
Dancing close, the warm sun beats,
In the chaos, joy's design,
Nature's humor intertwines.

At dusk, the fireflies gleam,
Painting laughter, such a dream,
In the shade of joyful trees,
Giggling whispers ride the breeze.

Cheerful Shoots in Sunlit Glades

In a nook where giggles blend,
Little sprouts peek round the bend.
They dance and twirl, with glee they sprout,
Making the bumblebees stamp and shout.

With sunshine smiles, they stretch so high,
Tickling the clouds in the bright blue sky.
A whimsy party, no one can miss,
As the butterflies join in for bliss.

Echoes of Childhood in the Woods

Whispers of laughter fill the glen,
Tiny green folks tease now and then.
Swinging on branches, they dive and roll,
Pretending to be the bravest soul.

With dandelions as crowns of gold,
They tell tales bold that never get old.
Running in circles, they laugh and shout,
Playing hide and seek, without a doubt.

Playtime in the Meadow's Shade

In the cool green grass, they plot and scheme,
Wiggling their roots in the sun's warm beam.
Chasing each other in a playful race,
With twinkling eyes, they savor the space.

Toadstools serve as seats for chats,
While ladybugs wear their little hats.
They giggle and bounce, oh what a sight,
As shadows dance in the fading light.

Lighthearted Greenery Frolic

Bouncing around, they sway with glee,
Whirling about, a jolly spree.
Each little leaf has a ticklish trend,
While branches above twist and bend.

In the meadow, games take flight,
As sunbeams twinkle, pure delight.
With laughter echoing, they spread the cheer,
As wildflowers whisper secrets near.

Emerging Life and Lively Play

Tiny shoots peek out with glee,
Wiggles dance in the breeze,
In this world of green delight,
Nature's giggles take their flight.

Roots entwine like old best friends,
While sunshine on their laughter blends,
Sprouts raise leaves in cheerful cheer,
Who knew dirt could bring such mirth here?

Innocent Growth and Laughter's Embrace

Under skies so wide and bright,
Little buds stretch with all their might,
Tickled by a playful breeze,
A chorus of tickled leaves and tease.

Wiggly tendrils wave hello,
Playful whispers start to flow,
Nature's jests, a silly race,
A joyful giggle fills the space.

Budding Happiness and Spirited Jests

Green fingers tickle soft and spry,
Clouds roll by, dancing high,
Laughter sprouts from every root,
Comedic leaves in funny suits.

Today the sun is extra bright,
Casting shadows that give a fright,
Round and round in nature's spin,
Each bump and tumble brings a grin.

Growing Worlds and Lighthearted Tales

In gardens where the giggles grow,
Every bloom puts on a show,
The breeze tells jokes to branches wide,
As laughter echoes, side by side.

Here a sprout, there a vine,
Every twist is grand design,
With playful sprites and happy claps,
Nature's fun with her little traps.

Echoes of Innocence and Playful Rejoice

In a garden where giggles roam,
Tiny sprouts make a silly home.
With wagging tails and little hops,
They tease the bugs and dodge the drops.

A leaf tickles an ant's parade,
While shadows stretch in a playful charade.
Each twist and turn a laugh's delight,
Nature's jesters in morning light.

The Lightness of Growth and Joyful Days

Watch the green sprites stretch with glee,
Doing cartwheels, carefree as can be.
Sunbeams tickle the tender shoots,
While clouds play hide and seek with roots.

Breezes whisper secrets, just for fun,
They swirl and twirl; oh, what a run!
Squirrels giggle, stealing the show,
As petals flutter in a frolic below.

Little Green Mirage and Laughter's Dance

Dancing buds in a playful race,
They trip and tumble, a leafy embrace.
The sun winks down with a cheeky grin,
As blossoms burst with a jubilant spin.

Each tiny sprout, a comedian's dream,
Juggling rain drops like a gleeful team.
In this whimsical realm of the light,
Laughter echoes, oh what a sight!

Fresh Beginnings and Merry Whispers

In soft soil where whispers blend,
Tiny tales of joy ascend.
With every stretch and playful sway,
Life sings sweet tunes of a bright new day.

A jolly breeze carries silly songs,
While worms wiggle to where humor belongs.
Nature chuckles as it gives birth,
To giggles and grins upon this earth.

New Life and Grinning Faces

From the ground, new sprouts emerge,
With tiny leaves, they start to surge.
Their roots tangle like silly shoelaces,
While sunbeams tickle all their faces.

A little breeze gives them a shove,
As if to say, 'Get up, my love!'
They sway and dance in playful glee,
Who knew plants could giggle so free?

The Dance of Sprouts and Chuckling Breezes

Tiny friends in rows so neat,
Twist and twirl on little feet.
They whisper jokes to one another,
'What's green and funny? A leafy brother!'

The wind assists with hops and skips,
While raindrops playfully kiss their tips.
They chuckle at the clouds above,
While dreaming of sunshine and love.

Flourishing Tales and Soft Giggles

In a world where green things sprout,
Funny tales are what it's about.
A daffodil tells a tree to 'shush!',
But the tree just laughs in a leafy hush.

The ants parade in silly lines,
As flowers giggle, 'Look, our designs!'
Each petal flutters in pure delight,
In this garden, life feels just right.

Cheerful Shoots and Boisterous Laughs

Up they pop, the shoots so spry,
With wide-eyed grins, they touch the sky.
They share their dreams with buzzing bees,
And spread their joy upon the breeze.

A root tickles a worm nearby,
With raucous laughter, oh so high!
In unison, they cheerfully sway,
Making the most of a sunny day.

Grounded Joy and Amusing Antics

In a garden full of glee,
Tiny shoots dance so free,
With the breeze they twirl and spin,
Where silliness grows from within.

Wiggly roots play hide and seek,
While squirrels chatter, oh so cheek!
A flower blushes, can you see?
It's laughing at the buzzing bee.

Pitter-patter, rain drops play,
Messy puddles come our way,
Watch the earth as it shakes and wobbles,
Oh, those giggles in the troubles!

Beneath the sky, a comedy,
Nature's jesters, can't you see?
With every sprout a little grin,
In this place, the fun begins!

Sproutling Dreams and Cheery Rhymes

Sprouts whisper secrets in the sun,
Tickling leaves, oh what fun!
Mischief hides in every fern,
A twist of fate, a comic turn.

Bright blooms borrow the sun's glow,
While crickets join in, stealing the show,
A twirling leaf gives quite a leap,
Laughter echoes, oh so deep!

Jumpy bugs engage in play,
They hop and skip throughout the day,
With every wiggle, a chuckle comes,
Nature's antics, oh so fun!

In a world of green and cheer,
Laughter sprouts, forever near,
With every clap of wind's soft song,
Life's a garden, where we belong!

Nature's Giggle and Playful Sunshine

A tiny sprig in sunshine's glow,
Tells a tale of joy in tow,
With each breeze, it starts to sway,
Tickling petals on its way.

Jolly critters race around,
Chasing shadows on the ground,
Those wiggly worms with no real plan,
A wobbly dance, a wild jam!

Bright daisies burst in laughter loud,
Claiming space, they feel so proud,
With every bloom, a joke unfolds,
Nature's humor, a sight to behold.

Beneath the sun, in vibrant hues,
Laughter mingles with morning's dues,
As nature giggles, we can't resist,
Join the fun, we simply must!

Laughter Beneath the Canopy

Under leaves, where shadows play,
Whispers of mischief come our way,
Beneath the boughs, the critters prance,
In this woods, all join the dance.

Bouncing berries roll with glee,
While nutty squirrels plot, oh me!
What a scene, how absurd,
A comedy script, you've heard?

Ticklish grasses sway and tease,
As playful winds weave through the trees,
In every nook and cranny found,
Laughter bubbles all around!

So find your joy where nature smiles,
Join the fun, stay a while,
In this comedy where all can see,
Every leaf shares a giggly spree!

Tender Greens and Lively Banter

In the garden, sprouts appear,
Tiny leaves with no fear.
They giggle in the sunny glow,
Making jokes that only they know.

A worm wiggles, doing a dance,
While the buds all take a chance.
Each chuckle spreads through the air,
Nature squeals without a care.

Playful Leaves and Heartfelt Laughter

Leaves rustle as the wind sings,
Jokes bloom like the first spring things.
A branch tickles the sky so high,
As clouds giggle and skip by.

With every twist, the flowers prance,
In a game of chance and dance.
Nature's humor fills the scene,
In this lively, verdant green.

Cherished Bloom and Joyful Glee

A bud pokes up, adorned in cheer,
Whispering secrets to all near.
It laughs as bees come buzzing round,
Sharing jokes without a sound.

The sun plays peek-a-boo each day,
Shooting rays in a playful way.
In this patch of colors bright,
Laughter echoes, pure delight.

Soft Earth and Mirthful Moments

Beneath the soil, a party brews,
Where critters crack some silly clues.
With roots that wriggle, dance, and sway,
They band together for a play.

The earth giggles with every sprout,
As the sun peeks in, no doubt.
A feast of joy, a garden wide,
With laughter blooming side by side.

Bright New Growth and Silly Smiles

Tiny sprouts peek from the ground,
They wiggle and giggle without a sound.
With each little shake and soft little sway,
They dance in the breeze, in their own funny way.

A worm tries a jig, slips under a leaf,
Laughing and wiggling, causing much grief.
The raindrops join in, with splashes and pops,
Creating a symphony as the laughter drops.

Little leaves quiver, trying to tease,
While twirling around like they're caught in a breeze.
The sun's golden grin lights up the scene,
While shadows play hide and seek in between.

Oh, what a party, nature's sweet jest!
With funny little plants, we are truly blessed.
Each bloom a chuckle, in wild disarray,
Bright new growth spreads joy in a playful way.

Innocence of Nature and Playful Jokes

In a garden where innocence dances with glee,
Frogs start a band, oh so splishity-splish they be.
With toads as the singers, their voices a hoot,
They croak silly tunes while wearing rain boots!

Bees buzzing loudly, with lines quite absurd,
Debating the flavors of nectar they've heard.
A flower wearing glasses shouts with great flair,
"I'm the smartest bloom! Less pollen? Beware!"

A butterfly flutters, showing off tricks,
Landing on noses, barely avoiding the licks.
In this joyous chaos, life's laughter erupts,
Even the daisies can't help but erupt!

Nature's a jester, with jokes fresh and bright,
In every small corner, there's pure delight.
From petals to critters, all join in the fun,
Innocent laughter beneath the warm sun.

Young Blossoms and Radiant Laughter

Young blooms break through with curious eyes,
Whispering secrets as the butterfly flies.
Each petal a giggle, each stem a light sway,
In joyous embrace, they welcome the day.

Tulips are tugging on daisies nearby,
"Do you hear the news? Let's give it a try!"
While pansies exchange their playful little grins,
Underneath raindrops, the laughter begins.

A squirrel with acorns is loading his stash,
Tripping and tumbling, oh what a crash!
The garden erupts in shouts of delight,
As critters create a most comical sight.

From morning to dusk, joy frolics around,
In each little heartbeat, silliness found.
In the heart of the garden, sweet mirth does grow,
Radiant laughter to brighten the show.

Gentle Greenery and Pleased Thought

In gentle green fields where mischief abounds,
Twinkling with joy, nature's laughter resounds.
A rabbit named Chuckle hops high with delight,
Chasing his shadow in the warm sunlight.

The daisies giggle in a cheerful array,
As butterflies whisper, "Let's frolic and play!"
"Who can spin fastest?" they giggle and tease,
With petals all swirling like a soft breeze.

With tickled green grasses that sway and bend,
The sun casts a grin, its warmth to extend.
The clouds bring a chuckle, as they drift near,
And nature's own jester spreads laughter and cheer.

Oh, why take it serious? Join in the fun!
With playful thoughts, let your spirit run.
In the waves of green, let joy take its flight,
As gentle greenery welcomes the light.

Little Greens and Joyful Chortles

In a garden full of cheer,
Tiny plants wave hello,
With the sun shining bright,
They dance to and fro.

Worms wearing tiny hats,
Join the cheerful dance,
Giggling with the breeze,
Giving roots a chance.

Ladybugs are laughing,
As they march in their line,
Tickled by the tall grass,
They feel just so fine.

With petals that are grinning,
And leaves that sway so free,
Nature's joyful party,
A sight that's fun to see.

New Roots and Playful Grins

New sprouts poke through the dirt,
With faces bright and spry,
They giggle at the raindrops,
Swooping from the sky.

In the patch of soft green,
They tell funny tales,
Of bees in tutu skirts,
Who jump and wiggle their tails.

Squirrels join the laughter,
Chasing friends around,
While dandelion seeds
Perform flips off the ground.

Rooted deep in giggles,
With sunshine all around,
Every day a party,
In this playful playground.

Growing Dreams and Silly Chuckles

In the warmth of bright sunshine,
Little sprouts begin to play,
With dreams of reaching high,
They frolic every day.

Wiggly worms with funny hats,
Join in on the fun,
Twisting through the soil,
Dancing 'til they're done.

Petals sway to music,
Composed by buzzing bees,
While raindrops play the drums,
Beneath the shady trees.

In this world of laughter,
Where all joy is esteemed,
Nature's great adventure,
Is wider than it seemed.

Fresh Shoots and Lighthearted Jests

Sprouts stretch up towards the sky,
With grins that burst with glee,
Cracking jokes with bumblebees,
A comic jamboree.

Ticklish leaves are shaking,
In a playful afternoon,
While branches weave a story,
In the soft light of the moon.

Frogs leap high with laughter,
In their carefree, silly ways,
While snappy snails on chunks of mulch,
Join in the frolic phase.

Every breeze brings giggles,
In this vibrant, lush fest,
Where every little creature,
Knows laughter is the best.

Nature's Cradle and Happy Murmurs

In the garden, things do grow,
With little plants in a row.
They wiggle and sway in sunlight's glow,
Tickling roots, as breezes blow.

A rabbit hops with a silly grace,
While gnomes guard their leafy space.
Their painted smiles can't hide the trace,
Of mischief found in every place.

A worm in shades of bright green hue,
Dances solo, what a view!
Nearby, a bird with a laugh so true,
Sings to the blooms with joy anew.

Nature's cradle rocks with cheer,
While critters gather, drawing near.
In whispers soft, they spread good cheer,
Planting giggles, year after year.

Sprouting Joy and Witty Whispers

Sprouts peek out with a yawn so wide,
While ants line up for the wild ride.
Frogs leap over, full of pride,
Telling tales of the river's tide.

A squirrel flips in a playful dance,
Finding nuts is quite the chance.
With every jump, it takes a stance,
And giggles echo, like a trance.

Atop a stump sits a beetle, stout,
With wise old tales, it brings about.
The laughter flows, there's never doubt,
In this green world, joy's a route.

With every seed, a story springs,
Of sunshine days and butterfly wings.
Through whispers shared, everyone sings,
Nature's laughter, oh how it clings!

Budding Life and Quick Quips

Buds burst forth in a sunny spree,
Critters scurry, oh what a glee!
A hedgehog spins, less careful than free,
Rolling down, past the old oak tree.

A chatty flower boasts of its looks,
As bees write poems in simple books.
With every buzz, mischief hooks,
Whisking laughter into the nooks.

Ducks quack jokes while wading in streams,
Splashing about in their fun-filled dreams.
Nature's comedy, bursting at seams,
Stitches joy with laughter's gleams.

With leafy branches swaying tall,
Echoes of giggles everywhere call.
In this garden, we're having a ball,
Growing together, we'll never fall.

Fresh Growth and Carefree Chuckles

Tiny shoots peek from the earth,
Laughing loud, they celebrate birth.
A snail slips by, oh what a mirth,
In the lively realm of green rebirth.

A breeze tells jokes to the leaves so bright,
While blossoms giggle until the night.
With every sway, they set the light,
Bringing cheer in the fading sight.

A comedic crow caws a big riddle,
While flower petals dance in the middle.
With butterflies playing a sweet fiddle,
Joy hums softly, never too little.

The sun dips low, day bids adieu,
While stars peek out, watching the crew.
Nature's laughter is always true,
In every bloom, in every view.

Vibrant Energy and Heartfelt Laughter

In a garden bright and merry,
Little shoots dance, oh so airy.
They wiggle, giggle, stretch with glee,
Chasing sunlight, wild and free.

Frogs wear hats, the birds all sing,
The flowers bask in springtime's fling.
With silly socks and playful shoes,
The fun is here; there's naught to lose.

Bouncing beans with capers bold,
Cracking jokes that never get old.
The breeze joins in, a jolly cheer,
As whispers of joy float out near.

Laughter blooms, a rainbowed sight,
In this whimsical garden, oh what delight!
Wiggly roots tap, dance on ground,
Where silliness and giggles abound.

Simple Joys in Emergent Life

Tiny buds burst through the soil,
Joking with worms, doing their toil.
Sunshine smiles, tickling their leaves,
Each whispering secret that life weaves.

Rays of warmth sprinkle the earth,
As roots have a party, oh what mirth!
The daffodils wear crowns of gold,
Chasing rainbows, feeling bold.

Puppies hop amidst the green,
Chasing butterflies, a joyful scene.
Nature giggles, oh what a sight,
Silly critters spread pure delight.

The robins paint stories in the sky,
As they joke and chat, fluttering by.
With each sprout, a smile does bloom,
In this cheerful space, there's always room.

Playful Sprouts and Cheery Revelations

A little sprout peeks from the ground,
With a quirky grin, oh such a sound!
Wiggling leaves, they clap and sway,
Beneath the sun, they dance and play.

The bees buzz in, doing a twist,
As flowers giggle, they can't resist.
With every buzz, a joke is told,
In a world where laughter unfolds.

Twirling vines with silly faces,
Create a laugh in secret places.
In this garden of hilarity,
Each plant shares its own clarity.

The breeze joins in for a wild ride,
With petals swirling, oh what pride!
The earth's a stage for playful fun,
In this radiant realm, joy's never done.

Joyful Flourish and Silly Soliloquies

Each new shoot bursts in delight,
Under the stars that twinkle at night.
Whiskered rabbits with jokes to share,
In the vibrant garden, life's quite rare.

Beetles wear glasses, strut with flair,
While grinning daisies throw in their dare.
Tales of laughter tumble and twine,
In the company of friends, all is fine.

Giggling fruits swing from the vine,
With mischievous minds, they conspire and shine.
The daisies giggle, the lilacs laugh,
As sunshine paints a joyful path.

A gentle breeze feels everyone's cheer,
In this lively place, joy's always near.
With vibrant hats and playful quips,
Nature's laughter gets joyous grips.

Tiny Roots, Big Dreams

In a garden, young shoots sprout,
Chasing sunshine, dancing about.
With tiny roots, they waver so,
Dreaming big, while winds gently blow.

Their leaves giggle at the rain,
Laughing softly, never a strain.
Whispering secrets to the bees,
Hoping to climb tall, with the trees.

With every breeze, a ticklish sway,
A troupe of greens in wild ballet.
They play tag with the clouds above,
Sprouting joy, like the flowers they love.

Oh, to grow, with laughter so bright,
Testing heights, reaching for light.
In this world, they bounce and beam,
Tiny roots with a mighty dream.

Joyful Growth in Playful Winds

Watch them wobble, those little greens,
Making mischief, causing scenes.
With every gust, they twist and turn,
In the breeze, they frolic and yearn.

They tickle each other with leafy tips,
Chasing shadows on playful trips.
Whispers of laughter dance on air,
A riot of growth with fun to spare.

They dream of heights, oh, what a sight,
Giggles echo in morning light.
Tiny branches stretch out to play,
With joyful growth leading the way.

In the garden where they all reside,
Nature's laughter is their joyride.
With every wiggle, they celebrate,
Life's a game, and they're first-rate.

Budding Smiles in Nature's Embrace

See the petals peeking wide,
Smiling brightly side by side.
Each bud's grin is quite a surprise,
Nature's humor before our eyes.

They sway and shake in the sunset glow,
Chasing shadows, putting on a show.
A chorus of giggles from bloom to bloom,
Unexpected joy in every room.

Sprouting laughter in every nook,
Tickling roots, like pages in a book.
With each giggle, they stand a bit tall,
Budding smiles, enchanting us all.

In this field of whimsy and fun,
Their playful dance has just begun.
Joyful blooms in every embrace,
Nature's laughter fills every space.

The Dance of Leafy Laughter

In the meadow, a party unfolds,
With leafy pals, laughter it holds.
Spinning round in a leafy craze,
They twirl together in sunny rays.

Breeze whispers jokes, and they come alive,
Leaping high, oh, what a vibe!
Poking fun at the bumblebee,
"Catch us if you can," they tease with glee.

Every rustle, a secret shared,
In this dance, nobody's scared.
With moonlit dreams and morning cheer,
They laugh harder, the end draws near.

So join the fun, and don't be shy,
With leafy laughter, we'll touch the sky.
Nature's giggle, a joyful trance,
Come join the dance, give it a chance!

The Joyful Embrace of Nature

In the garden, giggles bloom,
Tiny sprouts chase away the gloom.
Wiggly worms dance with delight,
As sunbeams play, oh what a sight!

Nature's jester, a blossom bright,
Tickles the air with sheer delight.
Butterflies flutter, wearing a grin,
While ants march on, a comical win!

Fragrant breezes tease my nose,
Like nature's breath, it softly flows.
A squirrel's leap, a silly spree,
As laughter echoes, wild and free!

Grasshoppers hop, a rhythmic beat,
With catchy tunes, they never cheat!
In this wild world, joy's decree,
Where every creature dances with glee!

Delicate Greens and Carefree Joy

In fields of green, the fun unfolds,
With every leaf, a prank retold.
Frogs make faces, silly and grand,
While dandelions dance, hand in hand.

Bumbling bees buzz their own tune,
Chasing flowers from noon to moon.
Each petal giggles, sways in the breeze,
Telling secrets to rustling leaves.

A cheerful tangle of twigs and vines,
Where mischief dwells among the pines.
Grass stains and laughter fill the air,
In this jungle of fun, free from care!

A chubby rabbit hops on by,
With floppy ears and a watchful eye.
A hop, a skip, a joyful jig,
In nature's arms, life feels so big!

Tender Leaves and Laughter's Song

Whispers of green in the soft, warm sun,
Where playful shadows skip and run.
A tiny sprout proclaims its cue,
'Come join the fun, there's room for you!'

Petals chuckle as the breezes tease,
While raccoons dance with mischievous ease.
With laughter spilling like a river wide,
Each gentle leaf wearing a grin with pride.

Giggling toads sing a croaky tune,
Underneath the watchful moon.
Nature's jesters, wild and free,
In every corner, joy's decree.

Sunset paints the sky in delight,
While critters prepare for a funny night.
In this world where laughter rings,
Nature, a stage where joy takes wings!

Blossoming Cheer and Bright Smiles

With petals bright, they share a laugh,
Dancing in sunlight, a vibrant craft.
Joy spills from the earth and air,
As playful critters scamper without a care.

Chirpy birds in a raucous choir,
Tickle the toes of branches higher.
In this world, where pranks are designed,
Laughter's nectar is always kind.

Boys with sticks chase shadows tall,
While gentle breezes make them fall.
Climbing trees, their giggles glint,
Flashing moments, no hint of tint.

So here we sit, on a fine green patch,
As laughter and nature lovingly match.
With every smile that the sun inspires,
Our hearts echo with playful desires!

Nature's Smiles Under Starlit Skies

In a meadow where the daisies dance,
Little sprigs play a silly prance.
With giggles echoing in the night,
They tickle the stars with pure delight.

Frogs join in with a croaky tune,
As fireflies twinkle beneath the moon.
The breeze whispers jokes, oh what a show,
Nature's comedy, always aglow.

A rabbit hops in a polka-dot hat,
Saying, "What's up with this big old cat?"
They laugh and roll without a care,
Under the sky's grand, twinkling glare.

The owls chuckle from tree-top heights,
While all the critters share silly sights.
In this playground of flora and fun,
Laughter amongst them has just begun.

Tangle of Joy in the Roots.

Twists and turns in the garden bed,
Wiggly worms make silly threads.
Each root tries to out-funny the rest,
A tangle of laughter, nature's jest!

Ants march in, their tiny parade,
With tiny hats that they have made.
They trip and tumble, oh what a sight,
Causing a riot in broad daylight.

Below the surface, secrets swirl,
As radishes giggle, giving a twirl.
Their tops peek out with a cheery grin,
In this leafy fest, everyone's in!

Sunshine spills on this cheerful crew,
With whispers and chuckles, all fresh and new.
In the roots, joy has found a way,
Producing smiles that brighten the day.

Tiny Buds and Gentle Laughter

Tiny green buds peek out to play,
Stretching their arms to welcome the day.
With soft chuckles like morning dew,
They break the silence, all bright and new.

The daisies gossip with cheeky tone,
While petunias giggle, never alone.
In patches where colors gleefully clash,
They burst into laughter—a vibrant bash!

Each bloom shares tales of the ones that grew,
Of sunlit days and drops of dew.
In this circle of buds, the joy's contagious,
Nature's laughter never feels outrageous.

As bees buzz by with their honeyed tune,
They listen close to the laughter's swoon.
In fields where flowers dance all day long,
Every breeze hums an ever-funny song.

Whispers of Sprouts and Sweet Giggles.

Whispers rise from the loamy ground,
Sprouts share secrets with a giddy sound.
A sunflower chuckles at joke-telling bees,
While leaves wave in the teasing breeze.

In the shady nook of leafy embrace,
Tiny critters have a tickle race.
The grass underfoot begins to sway,
In harmony with their playful ballet.

Shy tendrils curl in laughter's delight,
Wiggly roots share tales into the night.
With each little giggle, the garden thrives,
In a world where humor so brightly arrives.

So here in the soil, where joy runs deep,
Nature's little voices begin to leap.
With whispers and sprigs, this is the ticket,
To a garden of giggles, come join and pick it!

Nature's Play and Innocent Grins

In a world of green and giggles,
Where little sprouts peek out with cheer,
They tickle the ground with wiggly toes,
And whisper secrets for all to hear.

The sun beams down with a playful grin,
While clouds puff up like fluffy pillows,
A funny dance with a gentle breeze,
Makes giggles echo through the willows.

In the patch, where laughter grows tall,
A frog leaps high in a comical spree,
He jumps and croaks a silly tune,
As daisies sway with glee.

With every tumble and tumbleweed,
Nature crafts a joyful jest,
In the garden of chuckles, let us play,
Where the heart finds its zest.

Tenderness of Earth and Joyful Echoes

On soft, warm soil, new friends arise,
With funny hats made of leafy lace,
Each wave of green has a cheeky smile,
In the tender earth, there's a joyful place.

The worms throw parties under the ground,
While ants parade in a silly line,
With tiny trumpets and small tambourines,
They groove to tunes divine.

Bumblebees buzz like comedians,
In search of nectar, they share a laugh,
As they trip and tumble like little clowns,
Creating joy in their fragrant path.

Giggling flowers sway to the beat,
With petals dancing all about,
In this whimsical world that playfully thrives,
Nature's fun is what it's all about.

Little Wonders and Mirthful Memories

Tiny seeds with dreams so big,
Hatch into wonders, a dance so slick,
With each new sprout, a tale begins,
In a world alive with belly laughs and kicks.

Grass blades tickle tiny toes,
While butterflies play hide-and-seek,
With every rustle, there's a grin,
Laughter bubbles, cheek to cheek.

A curious critter peeks around,
With big bright eyes, he greets the morn,
The world is bright with things to see,
In the garden where joy is born.

So let's embrace this merry spree,
With all its quirks, its giggles, and grace,
For every little wonder out there
Leaves a smile on nature's face.

Echoes of Growth and Playful Revels

As the sun sneaks in with a wink,
New growth leaps up with flair,
A bouncy ball of joy on the rise,
Who knew dirt could hold such laughter in there?

The leaves rustle like giggly kids,
Playing tag with the gentle breeze,
A silly dance under the blue sky,
Makes the heart twirl with ease.

With sleepy roots that wiggle at night,
And blossoms yawning at the dawn,
Nature whispers secrets of fun and flight,
In every sleepy petal drawn.

As the day ends with chuckles and tickles,
The stars twinkle with slumber's grace,
In the world of growth where laughter thrives,
Every moment is a joyful embrace.

The Playful Spirit of Rising Green

In the garden, sprouts do jive,
Tiny leaves on a dance to thrive.
Wiggling roots and giggling buds,
Nature's chuckle, in happy floods.

A breeze whispers secrets so sly,
Watch them sway, oh my oh my!
Sunbeams tickle tender shoots,
They laugh in their fluffy green suits.

A cheeky worm on a leaf does slide,
As blurry bees begin to glide.
The merry chorus of new life sings,
Each note a jest that joy still brings.

With every sprout, a grin unfurls,
Nature's joke in bright twirls.
From earth below to sky above,
The playful spirit is full of love.

Nature's Chortle in the Springtime

Under the sun, the blooms erupt,
Tiny petals all tightly cupped.
They stretch and yawn, a bright display,
While ladybugs dance and sway.

Pollen sprinkles like joyful confetti,
Ants march by, in clothes so petty.
With every bloom, the giggles swell,
What stories these blossoms might tell!

Bumblebees buzz in a silly tune,
As flowers giggle beneath the moon.
The wind joins in, a jest so sly,
Nature's humor, oh my oh my!

A garden filled with playful cheer,
Brings forth laughter year after year.
Every petal and laugh set free,
Whispers of joy for you and me.

Frogs and Foliage: Tales of Fun

In puddles wide, frogs leap and play,
With slimy skin, they sing all day.
Between the leaves, they hide and seek,
Each croak a giggle, cheerful, unique.

Tadpole races, who will win?
They splash around, with toothy grins.
Among the weeds, they plot and scheme,
Nature's laughter, a hop and dream.

Under a leaf, a frog may snooze,
But wake him up? You'd get quite the ruse!
His bulging eyes, a comic sight,
In leafy realms, joy takes flight.

Join the fun, don't let it pass,
In every leap, in every grass.
Frogs and leaves, tales of delight,
In nature's play, all feels just right.

Beneath Blossoms, Laughter Grows

Beneath the blooms, a secret place,
Where chuckles hide and giggles chase.
The petals whisper stories old,
Of playful beings, brave and bold.

Roses wear a crown of jest,
While daisies caper, feeling blessed.
The bumblebees twirl in rounds,
Through fragrant air, mischief abounds.

In shadows cool, where laughter lingers,
Tiny critters with wiggly fingers,
Peek through leaves, their eyes aglow,
Nature's humor is all they know.

As daylight fades, the giggles rise,
In every shade beneath the skies.
A world of whimsy, merry and free,
Where joy takes root, for you and me.

Bright Moments in Blooming Underbrush

In a forest filled with green,
A squirrel wore an ice cream cone.
He slipped and slid right off the scene,
While giggling birds just laughed and shone.

A hedgehog danced on tiny feet,
With clumsy grace, he spun around.
The rabbits chuckled at the feat,
His prickles flew, they hit the ground.

Beneath the oaks, a tortoise rapped,
With tiny paws, he made a beat.
The creatures stopped, they clapped and clapped,
As he performed with cool finesse, neat.

A chipmunk juggled acorns high,
One wobbled down with comic flair.
It hit a frog who hopped nearby,
The forest roared with laughter, rare!

Leafy Laughter Under the Sky

A caterpillar, green and bold,
Tried on a hat three sizes too big.
It tumbled down, the crowd consoled,
As it rolled on, refusing to dig.

The bumblebees sang silly tunes,
While buzzing round the flowers bright.
They forgot how to fly too soon,
And crashed into a bush, oh what a sight!

A chubby mouse with cheese to share,
Invited all for snack and fun.
Each took a bite, then gasped in air,
That cheese was stinky, everyone!

The sun shone down, the leaves did sway,
As laughter filled the spacious green.
In every nook, the critters play,
A joyful world, so pure and keen!

Nurtured Dreams in the Quiet Soil

In secret spots where shadows creep,
A mole found cookies baked with glee.
He ate them all, then took a leap,
But tripped and tumbled by a tree.

A ladybug wore shades so cool,
She strutted like a dancing queen.
She slipped into a tiny pool,
While ants all giggled at the scene.

A playful fox with painty paws,
Decided he would sketch his friends.
He painted stripes with lots of flaws,
And ended up with zebra bends.

The sun dipped low, the night drew near,
Yet giggles echoed through the glade.
With every joke, they spread good cheer,
In soil where dreams and laughs were made!

Whispering Hilarity Among the Pines

Among the pines, a parrot squawked,
With jokes that made the woodpecker crack.
The pine cones fell, the ground they rocked,
As laughter winged like a cheerful snack.

A raccoon donned a mask of fun,
He fought a shadow like a knight.
But when he slipped, he came undone,
And rolled away in sheer delight.

Two owls blinked in crisp night air,
They hooted rhymes, and twists of fate.
Their words went round from stump to square,
Echoing through the woodland gate.

In every branch, in every nook,
The mirthful spirit came alive.
For nature's stage, a merry book,
Where critters giggle, thrive, and strive!

Cheerful Earth and Smiling Buds

In the garden of giggles, they sway,
Little sprouts laughing, come out to play.
With roots in the ground, they dance in cheer,
Whispering jokes that only they hear.

Sunshine tickles with rays of delight,
Dewdrops sparkle like stars in the night.
Wiggling worms join in with a laugh,
Telling tales of their wiggly path.

Nature's Tender Touch and Glee

Fluffy clouds drift, wearing big grins,
While squirrels are plotting their nutty wins.
Blossoms blush bright, it's a colorful jest,
Each petal a joke, nature's funny best.

The breeze has a chuckle, rustling leaves,
Whirling around like a friend who believes.
Rabbits jump high, just to spread the cheer,
Their ears flopping wildly, what a sight here!

Growing Grins and Joyful Breezes

Little green sprouts poke heads from the earth,
Sharing their laughter, that's real, not mirth.
Ladybugs dance in a wiggly line,
Telling the sun, 'Your shine is divine!'

With every tickle from soft, gentle winds,
The flowers burst open, joyful chins spin.
Bumblebees buzzing a comedic tune,
While butterflies flutter, prancing like school.

Cackles in the Garden

The tomatoes are rolling, giggling bright red,
While peppers crack jokes, you've got to be fed.
Cucumbers chuckle, hiding their green,
In this garden of fun, they're the laugh scene.

Carrots stretch high, trying to stand tall,
While onions, they giggle, they just want to bawl.
Every leaf shakes with laughter so free,
In this patch of joy, come and see!

Vibrant Greens and Mischievous Smirks

In the garden, laughter creeps,
A tiny leaf that slyly peeps.
Tickling buds with playful glee,
Nature's joke for you and me.

Foliage wiggles in the breeze,
Winking trees, all set to tease.
Bouncing branches, quite absurd,
Whisper secrets, never heard.

Petals dancing, feeling spry,
Silly shadows passing by.
With each breeze, a chuckle stays,
Brighten up our sunny days.

Sprouted smiles in cheerful hue,
Swaying lightly, just for you.
Greenery with a wink and nod,
Here's the joy with just a prod!

Little Leaves and Heartwarming Humor

Tiny sprouts with faces bright,
Sharing giggles, pure delight.
Rolling round in playful games,
Nature's laughter, calling names.

Wobbling stems beneath the sun,
Each green friend wants to have fun.
Joking petals start to sway,
In this park where kids can play.

Leaves are grinning, what a sight!
Chasing shadows, pure delight.
Little whispers on the breeze,
Ticklish roots beneath the trees.

Boundless joy from dirt below,
Every giggle starts to grow.
With each tickle from the ground,
Happiness is all around!

Growth and Joy Under the Sun

Beneath the sun, they stretch and leap,
With every wiggle, secrets keep.
Chasing rays, they race and prance,
A lively, leaf-filled summer dance.

Roots are laughing, breaking free,
Joyful chatter, can't you see?
Sprouts are plotting mischief mild,
Nature's antics, sweet and wild.

Giggling leaves in vibrant hue,
Hosting games for just a few.
Watch them twirl in playful cheer,
Under skies so bright and clear.

Tickled by a gentle breeze,
Joyful bursts in all they please.
With every laugh beneath the sun,
The spirit grows; life's just begun!

Springtime Mischief and Jovial Echoes

Oh, the sprouts in spring are sly,
With a gleeful, watchful eye.
Each new bud is up to tricks,
Hiding jokes and fun-filled kicks.

In this season, laughter blooms,
Jubilant shouts across the rooms.
Swinging branches, teasing breeze,
Every whisper puts us at ease.

Colors flash in daylight's grace,
As giggles dance and merrily race.
From the roots to leaves on high,
Once you start, you can't deny.

Mischief wraps the garden whole,
Lively antics take their toll.
Echoes of laughter fill the air,
Springtime mischief everywhere!

www.ingramcontent.com/pod-product-compliance
Lightning Source LLC
Chambersburg PA
CBHW051645160426
43209CB00004B/799